Profitable

by

Scott A. Gardner

Sharon —

This book would not
be possible without
your help & friendship.
Thank you so much!!!

Love,
Scott

Other books by Scott A. Gardner:

Recognized Expert Status
Membership Site Design

The author may have an affiliate relationship with some of
the links listed in the book. He may receive payment if
you make a purchase.

Published by Dark Raptor Press
PO Box 2242
Clay, NY 13041
www. DarkRaptor.com
sales@darkraptor.com

First print version December 2014

To all the hosts I've had, especially the bad ones. You taught me what not to do.

And to all the clients I've had, especially the patient ones. You helped me to learn and to grow.

TABLE OF CONTENTS

INTRODUCTION..1
WHAT IS HOSTING?...5
DON'T DO IT...11
TYPES OF HOSTING...15
THE ESSENTIALS..17
SIMPLE MATH...19
IT'S A BUSINESS – TREAT IT THAT WAY................25
UNDERPANTS GNOMES....................................27
MAKE A PLAN...29
VALUE...35
MARKETING: WHAT IT IS, WHAT IT ISN'T..............39
COMMODITY VS. BRAND...................................49
CUSTOMER SERVICE..55
CUSTOMER-CENTRIC PRICING.......................59
GET CLIENTS BY HAVING CLIENTS........................63
TEAM UP..65
TARGET MARKETS...69
TAKING PAYMENTS...71
MONEY MANAGEMENT.....................................75
PUTTING IT ALL TOGETHER.............................77
EXAMPLE...81
FINAL WORD...85
ACTION ITEMS...87
RESOURCES...89
FREE PREVIEW: MEMBERSHIP SITE DESIGN.........91
ACKNOWLEDGEMENTS.....................................101
REGISTRATION...103

INTRODUCTION

*"How **exactly** do I make money as a web host?"*

My name is Scott Gardner, and I've been running on-line services since before there was a World Wide Web. In the bad old days, we'd set up a dedicated 286 in the corner and run Bulletin Board System (BBS) software on it. My personal favorite was the Wildcat! BBS from Mustang Software. You could fit one or maybe two Hayes-compatible modems in the computer case. Or, if you were a business with thousands of dollars for equipment, you might have stacks of systems with multi-line modem cards in them. And of course, all of this ran on top of MS-DOS as the operating system.

My point isn't to sound like some old geezer, dreaming about the days of horseless carriages and outdoor plumbing. My point is this: I've done it. I've been in the trenches, where you want to be. If there's a mistake to be made, I've made it. Probably more than once, before I wised up. And I continue to host web sites, albeit in a highly streamlined fashion. I am not some guy who read a couple articles, bought a site template and started my own hosting business last month. I have a small number of hosting clients, and each one of them gives me an annual return on my investment (ROI) of about 3,000%. And that's just the money they pay me for hosting.

I run Agile' Marketing Services, where we specialize in helping entrepreneurs and small businesses maximize the return on their investments in marketing their businesses. But let me tell you something else I'm not. I am not a "make money on the Internet" guy. I am not someone selling a "get rich FAST!" system. I believe in charging a premium price for a premium product, backed by premium service.

This book will show you the business side of running a profitable hosting service. If you follow the process I've outlined in this book, then you too can run a profitable web hosting service. But make no mistake: this is a business, and you'll have to put work into it. Not digging-a-ditch work, but work nonetheless. If you are looking for a "proven millionaire system," or something requiring "NO work – NO investment – NO kidding!" then you're wasting your time reading this book.

As I write this book – September 2014 – if you plug the phrase "cheap web hosting" into Google, you get back over **18 million** hits in .2 seconds. How many of those sites are making money? Do you really want to try to compete at the bottom of the scale?

More of what this book won't give you: I will not be giving you a magic list of hardware, software and vendors. I will not be giving you the formula for the perfect web site, or the very best whatever (payment processor, computer chip, web design – take your pick of a thousand things) to use in setting up your business. Prisoners have dug their way out of jail using spoons. Cheerleaders hold car washes in empty lots using soap, sponges and a garden hose. I'm writing most of this book using a ball point pen, 3 x 5 cards and a composition book. You do not need specialized equipment, or just the right software, or a bullet-proof process. You need heart, dedication and determination. You need to be willing to work, to do the very best job you can, to fix your inevitable mistakes and to stand behind your services. You need to be willing to make current and potential customers happy. You need to learn just enough math to make sure you're making more money than you're spending. Most importantly, you need to learn to fix things that aren't working, make changes, and try again.

So what, exactly, will you get out of reading *Profitable Web Hosting*?

You'll be introduced to the down–and–dirty basics (I did not say "tricks") of actually making money as a web host. You'll be given a process that actually sets you up from the very start to make a profit from your very first sale. You'll be shown how to make mutually beneficial connections with other business owners. You will be shown several bits of information where you'll say "No kidding – everybody knows that," yet when you look around, you'll see that almost no one is using them! You'll get some easy-to-understand concepts that most other hosts completely ignore, which will keep your enterprise profitable while they go out of business. You'll be shown, in short, the way to market your hosting business.

And, if you're smart, you'll realize that these basics, this process, can be applied to any business, on–line or off, allowing you to "gain multiple streams of income" (that old Internet Marketer battle cry).

Why am I writing this book? Because every time I visit an on-line web hosting discussion area (my favorite is www.WebHostingTalk.com), I see the question from above over and over again. And I see the same people trying to provide a short, pithy, all–in–one answer over and over again, God bless 'em. To which the original poster almost always replies *"Yeah, but **exactly** how do I do that?"*

Not your fault, ye brave and valiant few who share knowledge on-line. I, too, used to smack my head against a wall offering free professional advice. Different media carry different psychological weights, and if it costs more, it must be better advice. Remember that when you're setting up your hosting business!

This book does not replace all the good advice available in on-line discussion forums. Again, there are lots of subjects this book can't and won't cover. Keep asking questions about servers and software and payment processors and listening to topical and sage advice. But keep this book on your desk and, when in doubt about what makes money in the web hosting business you're running, open it and re-read it, making sure you apply the techniques outlined here. If you've got the paperback, make notes in the margins. If you own the ebook, then highlight the passages you find the most valuable.

I wish you health, happiness and prosperity!

Scott A. Gardner

WHAT IS HOSTING?

If you want to be a profitable web host, you first have to answer the question, "What is web hosting?"

While the answer may seem easy and self-evident, rushing to a simplistic answer is like saying that all it takes to be a mother is to give birth to a child. Setting up hosting space on the 'net is analogous to a developer putting up an office building on a plot of land. Many developers have gone bankrupt from having beautiful buildings with no tenants.

Hosting web sites is a lot more than having space on a server attached to the 'net and putting up a sign somewhere that says "Great hosting this way." Running a hosting service requires a basic knowledge of hardware and software. It requires an idea of who your potential customer is and what they want from any hosting service. You need some knowledge of law as it pertains to the rights and responsibilities of both you and your clients. It requires a minimum of planning, and measuring the results of your plan. As I've said before, it's not digging–a–ditch effort, but it does require work.

Let's go back to our analogy of being a developer. You've built a building and now you want to rent out space. You can choose to pre–frame office and retail space, or you can court customers who want to specify the size and shape of the space they're renting. Some renters will want you to finish their space, while others may opt to do it themselves or even hire a 3rd party contractor. In any case, they expect you to offer some very basic services: utilities, plumbing, access to and from the building and some sort of security system even if it's just a lock on the front door. They expect you to have some sort of insurance in case of accidents or natural disasters. Most importantly, they expect to have someone to go to with their questions and concerns.

Potential hosting clients are the same way. They may want you to build their site if they don't do it themselves, or they may hire a web developer to do it for them. They expect that when they rent hosting, your server will stay up and be accessible to their audience . They want common infrastructure like a webserver, a control panel, and basic software like a database and email. They want to know that their site is being backed up somewhere on a regular basis and that if anything happens, it will be restored as completely as possible. And like renters in a building, they too expect to have someone to go to with their questions and concerns.

The Web (more properly, the World Wide Web) is just a part of the Internet. It was initially created as a way to display academic papers and then provide easy links between them. Originally created with just Hyper Text Markup Language (HTML) and text, the Web now serves up pictures, video, information stored in databases, and other interactive content using HTML, XHTML, PHP, CSS and other languages, platforms and utilities.

The Web has also changed from being primarily an academic resource to one used for commercial purposes. Just like in the physical world, businesses need a place to do business. On the Web, those places are web sites.

To expand on the analogy above, running a web hosting business is very much like being a real estate developer. You don't run your clients' businesses, but you provide the location (space) and auxiliary services to make it easy for them to run their business from your property. In real estate, some of these additional services might be regular and emergency maintenance, security, grounds keeping, and so forth. For web hosting, you also provide maintenance and security, along with other services.

At a minimum, you're providing space for the site, along with bandwidth. *Bandwidth* can be a difficult concept to understand. The term as used in web hosting can describe the amount of data transferred to or from the website or server within a given period of time, for example *bandwidth consumption accumulated over a month* measured in gigabytes per month. The more accurate phrase used for this meaning of a maximum amount of data transfer each month or given period is *monthly data transfer*. Bandwidth is really a measure of data transfer capacity, usually expressed in bits (or some larger multiple like kilobits, megabits or gigabits) per second. If all that is confusing, the following very silly explanation may help.

Imagine that you sold 1-inch round garden hoses. In addition to your monthly rent, your landlord charged you for every inch of garden hose that went in or out of the building. Let's say you had a two inch wide door, and it took one second per inch to transfer the hose. Let's also suppose the landlord was charging you one penny per inch of hose. That means, when a 100 foot hose was delivered to you, it would take 20 minutes (100 ft x 12 inches = 1200 inches, and 1200 seconds / 60 seconds per minute = 20 minutes) to get the hose into the building, and cost you $12 above and beyond what you paid the manufacturer. Now someone buys the hose, and it takes you another 20 minutes and $12 just to get it back out the door.

Things would be faster if you had a 3-foot wide door. Then you could make 3-foot wide coils (100 feet / 3 feet coils = 34 full or partial 1 inch thick coils) and get the hose in or out the door in just 34 seconds. A 100 foot wide door would allow you to move the hose even fast – just 1 second!

If you're moving that much hose, you could strike a deal with your landlord to have a certain amount of hose moving in and out of the building included with your rent. You only pay for hose by the inch when you exceed the amount on your lease.

This is pretty much the way bandwidth works in web hosting. The wider the door (pipeline), the faster things transfer back and forth. If large items like pictures and movies are viewed by visitors to your site, you'll need more bandwidth. Web hosts set a specific amount of bandwidth a site may use per month and then charge more when the site runs past that. Wireless phone companies do the same thing with minutes and text messages.

You might also provide the following hosting extras (some "extras" are more extra than others):

- Branded email
- Domain name registration
- Spam filtering
- Design tools
- Extra programs/scripts
- SSL certificates

●Database management programs

●Email list management software

Not every business requires all – or even some – of those extras, but they might want to know you offer them in case they ever do need them.

There are two major software platforms on which most web server software is run: Windows and Linux. Windows is a large operating system that runs on a Graphic User Interface (GUI). It requires a lot of computing power just to run the OS because of all the parts that are sitting there, ready to take over at a moment's notice, just in case a user runs a program that needs them. Linux (and all its flavors) are an offshoot of the UNIX OS, which is still a command-line based OS. True, GUIs have been coded for Linux, and you can run Linux using a GUI – I'm writing this book on a laptop running the Ubuntu distribution of Linux running the GNOME GUI. But Linux is generally smaller, leaner and therefore faster, leaving more of the hardware horsepower for the web server and all the scripts that each web site may call to run. It's safe to say that over 85% of the web sites running today are hosted on Linux machines.

A *script* is a special type of program that can be called on to perform tasks on a web site. A static web site can be thought of as a sort of digital brochure – it just sits there while you look at it. A dynamic web site often has one or more scripts which allow visitors to interact with the site; play videos, sign up for a newsletter by entering their e-mail address, whack animated moles which appear randomly in your browser window – you get the idea.

DON'T DO IT

I can give you a lot of misdirecting reasons why you shouldn't start a web hosting service.

- Running a business is a lot of work.
- There's more to it than meets the eye.
- It can cost a lot to get the business going.
- It's lonely work with long hours.
- The field is already crowded.
- Twenty-seven other reasons I'm not going to try to list.

The real reason you shouldn't start a web hosting business is this:

The world doesn't need another half-assed attempt at web hosting that will leave non-functioning "automated" sites and disgruntled customers in its wake. The 'net doesn't need another "service" whoring out (sorry, it really is the most appropriate term) hosting at $5/month with the first two – no, three – no, five! months free.

Statistically, web hosting "businesses" are started by people who spend too much time sitting in front of their computers and who think that they can make tons of money by doing no work whatsoever. After all, the whole process can be automated via software – you don't even need to anything but watch the money roll in to your bank account. These people believe that just because they've set up a site, the world will beat a digital path to their portal. When these geniuses realize that they actually have to **work** in order to get people to use their services, they get disinterested. They didn't realize it was a ***real*** business, and was going to take away from the time they needed to spend chatting/playing games/webcamming/blogging/whatever.

They don't even bother to take down their automated site, and so some schmuck comes along, looking for the very lowest pricing on web hosting, signs up, and gets hosed because there's no support, or no bandwidth or the server gets shut down a month after they pay for a year of service in advance.

I'm being mean, aren't I? I'm being rude, and my language is not fit for polite company.

Good. Take a hike. Really – put this book down and get lost. We do not need you starting up another web hosting service on the Internet. I and other real web hosting providers are tired of cleaning up these messes.

Running a successful business of any kind takes effort. It requires that you quit thinking about *your* wants and needs and think of your customers' wants and needs first. Shepherds know that if you take your flock to green grass, keep them fed and watered, fat and happy, they will not be as likely to wander away. In turn, you'll be rewarded with warm clothing from wool and food from the ever-growing flock. Ignore them, or treat them poorly, and they will leave you cold and hungry.

If you are not prepared to treat this like the business that it is, if you are not prepared to actually work at running your business, please don't start. You are doing more harm than good.

What, still here? You want another reason? Fine. Most people who start a web hosting service (it's not a real business until you treat it like one) refuse to do any research about the industry and then ignore all the advice they've solicited. They waste time and bandwidth asking age-old questions, ignoring good advice that was posted last week because "it's already out of date."

These are the unwelcome know-it-alls who muddy the water for everyone else. These are the "civilized" people who blunder into "primitive tribes" and promptly get shot with poison arrows, asking "Why?" as they lay dying in the jungle. Why? Because they're dangerous! They scare away game, tramp through gardens destroying food, and bring disease and madness with them. They think their lack of knowledge is actually a good thing.

If you persist in starting a web hosting service in this way, you will be reviled by all those around you – other hosting providers, people you ask for advice, soon-to-be-ex-clients – everyone.

But. . .

If you read this book, learn the lessons and make a serious attempt at applying them to the way you run your business (and once again – it is a business, and there is work involved), then you might have a chance at sticking around and making money.

TYPES OF HOSTING

There are several different types of hosting systems. While this book concentrates on running a profitable business based on reselling shared hosting, it's important to know about other systems as well. You may find yourself quickly outgrowing your reseller account and searching for clients able to pay you even larger fees to host them on larger, more powerful systems with fewer (or no) other users sharing the resources. At least, we hope your business keeps growing and becomes even more profitable! But let's start at the beginning.

Reseller Account – Shared Hosting

This is the analogy used in the last chapter. Someone else buys and manages the actual hardware and low-level hosting ability, but they lease you some of their space and bandwidth, which you in turn partition and re-lease. This is the simplest base for your web hosting business and least expensive start-up option. This is also the business model crowded with the most competitors. But remember, we're going to show you how to change the rules and remove most or all of your competition so don't get discouraged!

There can be hundreds, and probably thousands, of individual web sites running on one server. They share resources in order to run – RAM, the processor and access to the hard drive and the ports in and out.

Virtual Private Server (VPS)

In this case, you lease space on a larger server, and the owners create a special space just for you. They dedicate a certain amount of disk space and bandwidth to you just like with a shared server, except that it isn't shared. In effect, they build a self-contained server with its own IP address, RAM and processor access just for you, and then they build virtual walls around it, blocking you off from "the great unwashed masses." You can then either partition this space yourself or provide it to one client who's looking for a larger space and more computing power for their site.

Many VPS providers offer you the option of either unmanaged or managed VPSs. That is, either they will leave the system blank and you can set up your own OS and management system, or they can do that for you. While a managed VPS costs more, the extra expense from a reputable company makes it easier on you and better for the end user.

Leased or Co-located Server

Another option is to lease or buy the entire server, and it's all yours to do with as you will. But you pay another company to provide you a location where the server can be connected to power and Internet access. Usually, the co-location company doesn't provide you with management services but may make their technicians available on a pay-per-task basis. This is by far the most expensive option, but it provides you with the most control and greatest potential for profit. You can lease out your hardware and bandwidth to other resellers or directly to end users.

But as that web slinging super hero learned, with great power comes great responsibility. If the power goes off or the server locks up in the middle of the night, you're the one who's going to get the angry phone calls, and it's your responsibility to make everything right.

THE ESSENTIALS

In order to run a successful – that is, profitable – web hosting business, there are a number of things that are essential.

You need:

- An idea of whom you're going to serve (your target market)
- Enthusiasm
- A desire to work and provide value to yourself and others
- Time to run a business
- Some education (may we not so humbly suggest that this book provides quite a bit)

The business needs:

- A plan
- A process (outlined in the plan)
- An ISP (Internet Service Provider – how you get on the 'net)
- An upstream provider
- Email and phone
- Prospects
- A first client
- Trusted peer advisors
- A way to take payments
- A way to measure success (minimal bookkeeping)

Lots of businesses are run with less than these essentials, but most which last long enough to succeed have at least these.

Notice I didn't list "Luck" as something you need. Yes, fortunate breaks can be extremely helpful. However, it's been said over and over again, "You make your own luck." Thomas Edison once said: "Success is 10% inspiration and 90% perspiration." Gather the essentials, and you'll be well on your way to making your own luck.

SIMPLE MATH

In order to understand how the Profitable Web Hosting system works, you need to understand a little math. C'mon – don't be afraid! It's really very easy, and once you get it, you'll be able to grasp the whole system and apply it to making plenty of cash for yourself.

Profit is the money you have left over after you use your income to pay your expenses. Expenses are all the things you have to pay for.

EXAMPLE #1 – TARGET NUMBERS

Target numbers are just the numbers you want to achieve. Let's say you want to make a one–time goal of $1,000. So. . .

Target = $1,000

Now we need to figure out how to hit that target. If we sell something for $5, how many customers does it take for us to get $1,000?

1000/5 = 200

That is to say, $1,000 divided by $5 per customer equals 200 customers. We need to find 200 customers willing to pay us $5 each so that we have $1,000 in our hand.

But what if we raised our price to $50?

1000/50 = 20

Then we only need to find 20 customers. But what if we want to hit our target number with one shot?

1000/1000 = 1

If we can get just one person to pay us $1,000 we will have made our goal. Does this seem unreasonable? You may be thinking, "No one would pay that much for web hosting!" Not so – many companies pay several times that for hosting every single month! But let's not get ahead of ourselves.

EXAMPLE #2 – LOSS

Let's say that regardless of what we charge, we're able to find enough customers to bring in exactly $1000. Great! But our expenses – the money we owe others – is more than that. We owe $1,200 in expenses.

Income	$1,000
Expenses	$1,200
Total	$(200)

Even if we don't actually send the money out, we're operating at a net loss of $200. We owe more money than we're able to pay with our income. Do this for very long, and you will wind up bankrupt.

EXAMPLE #3 – BREAK EVEN

Let's say our income exactly matches our income. We're now breaking even – we can pay all our bills, but we don't have any money left.

Income	$1,000
Expenses	$1,000
Total	$ 0

If you have no money, you can't expect to cover any emergencies. Regardless of what business you're in, there are always unexpected expenses, trust me.

EXAMPLE #4 – PROFIT

Through hard work, we've been able to increase our income. Let's say our income is now more than the amount we owe others. The money that's left over is called the profit.

Income	$1,200
Expenses	$1,000
Total	$ 200

Remember, these were all one-time examples. The goal is to keep generating a profit month after month, year after year. The Profitable Web Hosting system gives you a way to do this if you follow it and apply it.

What good is profit? On a personal level, it can help you take trips or contribute to your family, even buy those things you've had your eye on, all without taking away from what the business needs to keep going and paying its bills. You could also re-invest that money back into the business, paying for upgraded services you can then offer to your customers, a larger monitor, and so forth. And remember to set some money aside for those unexpected expenses!

We've been talking a lot about expenses, but what are they, exactly? There are actually two kinds of basic expenses: *fixed cost* and *variable cost*.

Fixed costs are easy to understand because no matter what you do, they stay the same. Let's say you rent office space for your web hosting business, and let's imagine that the space costs you $500 per month. If you go in every single day, it costs you $500 for that month. And if you only visit the office three times, it still costs you $500 for that month. You can have 100 people in your office, or just yourself, and the rent doesn't go up or down. It's a fixed expense.

Variable costs, on the other hand, can fluctuate depending on a number of factors. You only need to pay for gas when you drive your car. If it's just sitting in your driveway, it doesn't cost anything to run. Buying printer ink or toner is a variable expense, because the more you use the printer, the more money you have to spend on the consumables. Variable expenses go up or down depending on how much of a product or service you use.

Every business has expenses. But in order to be able to plan and set goals, we'd like to know as exactly as possible what those expenses are going to be, month to month. Ideally, we want to maximize the fixed costs and minimize the variable costs in order to accurately gauge what we need to do to meet our income goals.

Some of the normal expenses you'll have while running a web hosting business include:

- A computer
- Your ISP bill
- Space and bandwidth leasing
- Minimal office supplies (folders, paper clips, etc.)

Some of the many possible extra-cost expenses include:

- Web design software
- A web designer
- Merchant account or other credit card processing fees
- Dedicated IP for e-commerce
- SSL certificate for e-commerce
- Paid support (for you, your clients, or both)
- Software licenses
- Marketing materials
- A good quality chair

Some of these expenses are fixed cost, and some are variable. Again, you want to make sure as often as possible you know how much money you'll need each month.

THERE ARE ONLY 2 WAYS TO INCREASE PROFIT:

1. Increase income
2. Reduce expenses

IT'S A BUSINESS – TREAT IT THAT WAY

There's an important difference between a business and a hobby. With a hobby, you can take it or leave it. Do it or don't. It's just for your enjoyment, and no-one else is affected if you decide not to do whatever it is for two months.

Running a business, though, is very much like having a child. It requires almost constant time, care and attention. The business, like a child, requires you to provide "food" (customers who want the products or services that the business offers), money, education and safety. A business requires your full attention, whether you feel like doing it or not.

The main focus of a business is to produce a profit from whatever it is that the owner does or produces. As I said before, *profit* is the amount of cash left over when the business' income exceeds its expenses.

We covered them in depth in the last chapter, but essentially *income* is the money that your customers pay you, and *expenses* happen when your business pays out money.

If you want the information in this book to work for you, you must treat your web hosting venture as a business, not a hobby.

UNDERPANTS GNOMES

There is an episode of Matt Stone and Trey Parker's wonderful animated series *South Park* where the boys contend with disappearing underwear. It seems that their shorts are being stolen by the Underpants Gnomes.

The gnomes have a business plan of sorts:

> 1 Steal underpants
> 2 ?
> 3 Profit!

They have no idea how to transform the mountains of undies into profit, but they have faith it will happen.

I get requests like this all the time: "Build me a website; I want to be a millionaire." When I ask what they base the final result (lots of money) on, they say it's because they'll have a web site. They view a web site as some magical, money making machine.

In order to make money and turn a profit (they are not the same thing), there must be something done with or to the underpants (web site). There must be some type of commerce involved. There must be some type of work performed.

Back in the late 1990s, I read a number of business plans for the burgeoning Web-based business industry. There was one famous plan that said essentially, "We'll give away bags of dog food and make a ton of money." When asked how exactly they'd make money, the answer was, "We'll send the bags by FedEx." That's an expense, not an income, and still not an answer.

Of course greedy, senseless venture capital firms backed these dill weeds and hundreds of others like them, and what we got for their efforts was the inflation and bursting of the dot-com bubble, plus stacks of expensive furniture in warehouses around Silicon Valley.

A question mark is not a plan. Starting up a web hosting service is not a license to mint money nor a magic machine which will do it for you. You must have a realistic plan that lays out, in detail, why you're in business and what you'll do for your clients so that they'll pay you.

MAKE A PLAN

Any plan is just like a road map. "I'm here, I want to get there, and this is how I'm going to do it." That's the basis, and from there it can become very complex if you're trying to write a business plan for becoming a major corporation. Your plan doesn't need to be very long, or very complex, at least at first. You could write your first plan on the back of a bar napkin.

A good business plan should be alive; it should change and grow as time goes on. The only way this happens is if you continually have it in front of you, are consulting it, making changes and recording every place you've been and where you want to go next.

The very first thing in making a business plan is setting a goal. It will probably start out very general ("I want to make a lot of money" is the first goal a lot of new hosting providers have) and should very quickly become focused and specific. "In five years, I want a home and family in Wilton Springs. The house will cost about $200k and I'll buy it with the earnings from my hosting business." The first example ("a lot of money") is really a wish. The second is a goal.

Next, you need to know where you are now. Again, a phrase like "I'm broke" is no good. Specifics are best: "I'm 20, unemployed and share an apartment in Podunk Corners. I've had a series of food service jobs, but it's not a career I'm interested in. I like going out to dinner and dressing well, but I don't have the money to do that. I have a high school diploma and want to get a college degree in sociology."

So far, so good. Now, you need to start sketching out the road map you'll follow to get from where you are to where you want to be. If you were driving across the country, the trip would take several days. For that trip, you'd want to break the big trip down into little trips of a day each. It's the same thing with your business plan. You might break it down something like this.

Getting Started
1. Name the business
2. Decide on target market
3. Write marketing plan
4. Choose type of hosting to be offered
5. Choose type of service I'm buying
6. Register hosting service URL
7. Contract for hosting service space
8. Design sales site

        Custom?

        Template?

9. Hook to payment processor & test
10. Start offering hosting packages as per marketing plan

These decisions set up some mini-goals, like securing your first 10 clients, providing enough service to get a testimonial, and creating a referral program. It's like setting up places you want to visit on Day One of your cross country trip. Once you've taken the first steps, it's important you keep challenging yourself to find new things to do. It's easier to get lazy after a success than after a failure. You'll want to take a couple days off, and the next thing you know you're broke again, and you have to start over at the beginning.

As you go along, keep setting larger and larger personal goals for yourself: a bigger monitor, and then a faster computer. Better roommates, then a small apartment with no roommates, that sort of thing. In between, you'll set and meet career goals the same way: host a local not–for–profit agency's web site, get mentioned in the local media for your service to the agency, then have them recommend you to a for–profit company and turn a profit. You'll "set the dots" for yourself, and then you figure out the actions you need to take to "connect the dots."

As the above example list shows, you'll also need a marketing plan. This is often a separate document for larger companies, but at the beginning you can (and should) tuck it right inside your business plan.

For the purposes of this book (which, in case you forgot, is called *Profitable Web Hosting)*, the important part of your business plan **is** the marketing plan section. The main business plan will guide you in running your hosting business. As you'll see in the next chapter, many businesses are dead but don't know it because the owners see money coming in the door every day and assume they're doing well. Just because the corpse is twitching, they think they've got a live body.

Marketing can be a complex subject. There are a couple chapters later on where we really go into this, but for now, I'm going to define marketing as ***anything you do to promote your company, products or services in a positive manner to your customers, potential customers, peers and the general public***. That said, the main goal of marketing for an entrepreneur or small business is to bring in enough revenue to make a profit. All of the other marketing aspects, such as public relations, branding, etc. arc a by-product of your sales efforts.

The very basics of a marketing plan should include:

1 Research possible client groups
2 Set target market
3 Define products and services you'll offer targets
4 Research other companies offering similar products & services
5 Create a multi-touch sales plan
6 Set pricing (covering cost for entire sales process and making a profit)
7 Start implementing the sales plan

The idea of a multi-touch sales plan or process is extremely important, and we'll go over it in detail in the later chapters. For now, just realize it *is* a process and that potential customers are not likely to rush to do business with you the first time they see marketing materials from your company.

Writing a business and marketing plan seems like a huge job, I know. The first trick is to break it down into little steps. The second trick is to constantly check and re-check that you're headed for your goals. You may change some of the major steps along the way (from hosting gaming sites to hosting sites for mid-size corporations, for instance), but don't let the changes stop you. By the way, it's okay to change your goal as you go along. You may find that you have the house and family in four years but don't want to give up hosting just yet. That's okay, just set a higher goal!

One final thought: *Your business plan is not just for you.* As you grow and change, there are many people who you may wish to share your plan with. If you're looking for a business loan, the bank or other lending institution will want to see what you've got. If you're looking for credit from a major vendor, they'll probably want to see your plan as well. Looking for a partner, or to sell your business? The other party will definitely want a well-developed plan – much more detailed than we've gone over here. Sometimes a major potential customer will want to look at your plan; they may want to make sure your goals are compatible and that you're both headed in the same direction.

Having a plan in place during expansion is important as well. When bringing on new people – be it a relative, an employee, and independent contractor or a college intern – a plan will help them understand what the business does, and what's expected of them, as well as help you outline their tasks and set goals.

Finally, having a business plan that's viewable by other parties is a sort of test or mark of your professionalism and success. If you're serious about running your hosting service as a business, you'll spend the time to plan where you want to go and how you're going to get there.

That's why a plan is a living document; it will change and grow along with your business. It allows you to set goals, measure your success and re-align your systems and processes to match your business' growth.

VALUE

Even in business, the value of a product or service is not solely about money. Value is often measured by the usefulness or desirability of something. As such, the concept of "value" is subjective rather than objective. That is, it means something different to each person considering it, and that meaning can change as time, place and situation change.

I'm going to use an extreme set of examples. You might think them ridiculous, but hang with me. I promise that there's some important information here.

Let's say you're stranded on a deserted island. There's no food, no fresh water and no way to get off the thing. You're sitting there wondering what to do when suddenly a bag falls from the sky and lands at your feet. Inside, you find 1,000 gold coins.

What's the value of the coins? Take a minute and think about it.

Nothing. Nada. No value whatsoever.

You can't eat them. You can't drink them. They won't keep you warm or dry. There's nowhere to "spend" them, and no food, clothing or shelter to "buy" anyway. They have no value on a desert island.

Well, you just need to get them to the main land, and you'll be rich!

Try swimming with them, and you'll get pulled to the bottom of the ocean. There's less than no value to them, actually. You're lucky they didn't land on you when they fell from the sky and kill you, which they certainly will if you try to carry them while swimming.

Imagine someone taking a poll of random people and asking "Is there anyone who wouldn't take a bag of gold?" Your hand would shoot up pretty fast.

Now imagine being asked, "What would you give me to rescue you from that desert island?" You'd offer them some of the gold. Why only "some?" Because the gold now has a *value to you*. You can give some to your rescuer and when you get back to the main land, other people will want the gold you have and will trade you all sorts of things for it.

The value comes from the usefulness – paying your rescuer – and the gold's desirability back among other people, who want it from you.

You come back from your desert island and decide to use some of your remaining gold to start a web hosting business. Congrats! You have something to trade – space and bandwidth – for cash (or chickens or office space – whatever).

The only people who want web hosting are those that value it. If they don't need to have a web site, they don't need hosting. No matter how low your price, there are people who simply will not buy your services. They don't need them.

"Aha," you say, "I'll offer them something of extra value if they buy their hosting from me." Since you happen to think hedgehogs are neat animals and can't imagine living without one of the spiny creatures as a pet, you offer a free hedgehog with every hosting sale. For some reason, people still are not beating a path to your door to buy hosting. Why not?

Because value is subjective!

What *you* think of as "valuable" is of no concern to your potential customers whatsoever. You must offer them something **they** value.

Back to the real world. . .

If you intend to offer something for sale (like web hosting packages), you need to find out what your potential customers value. How do you do that? Ask them.

You can contact potential customers and ask them a few questions, such as:

> • Do you need web hosting?
> • Do you already have a hosting provider?
> • What features do you expect in a hosting package?
> • What's the most important feature?
> • What's the least important feature?
> • If you have one, why did you pick your current host?
> • What would make you change to a different host?
> • What's your ideal hosting package consist of?
> • How much would you expect to pay for that package?

By their answers to your questions, you can find out what's

valuable to them. Maybe they want a low price. Maybe they want 24/7/365 service. Maybe they want extra bandwidth. Decide what you can offer them and match those features with those who desire and can pay for them. Suddenly, you'll find those paying customers of value to you.

No matter what, you must offer value to potential customers to get them to buy from you. You can use what others value to segment them into groups of people that will either be interested in what you're selling, or not interested, depending on what value you're offering.

MARKETING: WHAT IT IS, WHAT IT ISN'T

I gave you my definition of "marketing" in an earlier chapter (Make A Plan):

Anything you do to promote your company, products or services in a positive manner to your customers, potential customers, peers and the general public.

I think one of the best ways to look at marketing is like a soup that's been on the stove all day or simmering in a slow cooker. You can tell by looking at it that it's made up of different ingredients, but the flavors have melded and now complement one another.

Another reason I'm using the soup analogy: soup is made using a recipe, and a recipe is just a special type of plan. (If you haven't figured it out yet, I'm big on making and following plans.) A recipe is not just a list of ingredients, but it's also a process for combining and cooking them, as well as a goal for how the finished product should look, smell and taste.

Ingredients can be combined in different amounts, based on how you want the final product to come out. Still, if you're making split pea soup, you don't use carrots as the major ingredient.

Marketing, in general, is made up of the following components:

- Sales
- Finance

- Public Relations
- Promotion
- Research and Development
- Creative
- Advertising
- Strategy
- Production
- Distribution
- Customer Service

I believe that Sales is the most important component and Advertising the least important, especially for entrepreneurs and small businesses.

Larger businesses often have whole departments for marketing, and then departments for the different components. It's my experience that the people in different departments hate working with each other and consider these different departments as adversaries rather than allies. They work against each other and undermine the entire marketing effort.

Various "gurus" have competing ideas of what makes up marketing and what doesn't, which of the above disciplines are "included" in marketing, and which live in their own houses, so to speak. Here's my take:

Every person in a business is engaged in marketing. If they're not marketing – promoting the business in a positive way – they need to be eliminated. In large organizations, that goes from the president down to the people in the mail room and even the "custodial engineers."

So let's go over those departments/disciplines/components, shall we?

Sales

This is the beating heart of any business, especially for DBAs, mom-and-pop shops, and other tiny self-reliant firms. You got no sales, you got no nothing else. (I'm using the poor grammar for emphasis.)

A business (see the earlier chapter It's A Business – Treat It That Way) is, by definition, a profit making enterprise. You can't do good works, employ your friends and family, donate to charity or even put a roof over your own head and food in your belly until you start making sales.

This means that, as a corollary to my previous statement about marketers: *Everyone in your business from the top to the bottom should be an active sales person. If not, they need to be let go.*

Finance

The larger a business is, the more complex the flow of money becomes. Marketers need to make sure that their income exceeds their expenses. You can never lose sight of that rule. With Agile' I try to get the most effective marketing for my clients with the least amount of their money. The rest goes in my pocket. Why? Because my aim is to make Agile' a profitable business by making my clients' businesses successful.

Public Relations

Spin doctors. No, not the musical group. In large organizations, PR is handled by specialists who are half copy writer and half lawyer. They know exactly which words to use and which not to. They try to get your company covered by the media through means fair and foul. When there's bad news, they try to "spin" it so that the company comes out looking good.

You need to promote your company to the media, help them get the most flattering view of your company and find valid news items to report about you.

A lot of people stop there, thinking, "I can only use the media – newspapers, TV, E-zine publishers, bloggers, etc." They forget that this is **Public** Relations – so go ahead and find a way to talk to your public. Write your own releases, make your own news report videos and publish your own newsletter, either digital or print. You want to get complimentary information in front of customers, peers, and the general public. Do whatever you have to in order to make it happen.

Promotion

"Hey, let's put on a show!"

Promotion can be defined in different ways, but it comes down to an entertaining public action that somehow features your product or service. It may be as simple as announcing a sale on your products or distributing coupons that a person must present to a retailer to get a discount. It could be an attractive young woman talking to you in a bar as long as you buy her a shot of the premium vodka she's there to promote. It could be an infomercial that shares delicious recipes with you that taste best when used with their kitchen appliance.

Or, it could be you standing up in front of a group of people from your target market, giving a presentation on how a hosting feature you happen to provide with your service is essential for the well-being of their businesses.

Research & Development

R&D doesn't take a huge budget, and is not only for companies engaged in manufacturing. You can research what other companies are offering, and develop a product or service to either compete directly with them or better yet to address areas no one else is addressing. You should be doing this on a regular basis, before you start losing sales to someone else.

Creative

In larger companies and ad agencies, the Creative department is home to the artists and writers. Depending on the business, these people may also design packaging for products (and sometimes services). These are the people who dress funny and have funky hair colors, who get paid to imagine and dream.

Baloney. Everyone in your organization needs to be thinking and dreaming all the time, asking "What if?" and coming up with silly answers. Then they should report all their crazy ideas to the person in charge. If you've got good artists and writers, be humble and use them, even if their main job is to sweep up.

If your business and the people in it are *not* creative, it's probably not changing and growing. And that's a death sentence.

Advertising

Most people think the purpose of advertising (paid placement of a company's information in front of an audience) is to make sales. It isn't. Most advertising that attempts to make sales is poorly conceived and executed in an even worse fashion. This is a harsh thing to hear, I know.

I tell my clients that most advertising produced on less than a regional level is masturbatory: it feels good, but produces nothing.

The goal of good advertising is to create and emphasize your brand. It can be used to draw people in (to a bricks-and-mortar store, an on-line store or someplace else), but there they should be met by a salesperson (in person, on the phone, or via a professionally written sales letter). Only sales people make sales – nothing and no one else.

An ad that draws well will have a time-limited offer and convey a sense of urgency, along with telling the prospect something they either didn't know or had forgotten.

With my clients, advertising is the very last thing I recommend for them. If they decide to do it, I make sure they have all their ducks in a row and realize that advertising isn't magic. They will need to create a process by which they draw people in and have their sales professionals sell to the prospects.

If you're going to advertise, you must have a sales process in place and touch each prospect multiple times. In our media-rich society, *a person must see an ad on average of seven times before it sinks in*. Even then, there's no guarantee they'll take action on it.

Strategy

Strategy is *not* the exclusive province of crusty old men in suspenders sitting in board rooms smoking cigars. It's you, setting the big picture for your hosting business, writing out your initial or revised plan for success. It's the big map of where you are, where you're going and how you want to get there.

Production

Production isn't limited to physical product. Services like web hosting have a production aspect, too. The final product can be either factory made (accounts and sites set up, populated and enabled via automated software) or hand-crafted (all steps done by a live person).

Like physical production, web site production depends on raw ingredients ("Do we have enough space? Bandwidth?") in the pipeline. Someone also needs to pay attention to low supplies ("We have a bandwidth hog – better order more."), and cost of goods. Production isn't just about the finished product being delivered. Controlling production means not producing more than is needed, not buying more raw supplies than can be turned into salable finished product or service. Controlling production also means making sure the tools used in production are in good working order. ("That monitor is failing. Have we made back-ups of the data lately?")

Distribution

If you have blinders on then, yes, web hosting service is distributed exclusively via the 'net. But if that's how you're looking at your business, then you're missing a lot of business.

Do not dismiss the importance of face-to-face selling or of hand-delivering the results of your services. What can you deliver? I'd start with a printout of the server's "all set" message, usually showing site URL, log-in name and password, ftp information and so forth. I'd add a printed and signed version of the hosting contract. If you've created any site content, a printout of the code looks damned impressive, especially if the person looking at it has no idea what it means.

Of course, instead of hand delivering all this paperwork, you might send it out. You don't have to spring for overnight delivery (unless you want to – it's still very impressive), but you might consider sending the docs via USPS Priority Mail. Your mail will stand out, and most people will be happy to see you care enough about them to provide "rush delivery."

Customer Service

Customer service staff is second in importance to the sales staff. Everyone in your organization is directly involved in customer service. Except that most people deny it.

I can point you to several large corporations that spend millions of dollars annually to tell the public how wonderful their products and services are, and yet they are sabotaged by staff who interact with the public in inappropriate ways.

I refer you to a book entitled *Zingerman's Guide to Giving Great Service*, by Ari Weinzweig. It's just over a hundred pages. Grab a copy for each person in your business (especially yourself) and read it.

For years I've been telling people "The customer is always right" is BS. It doesn't matter if they're right or not. The statement you should live by is, "The customer should always be happy." The most successful businesses are famous for this.

Weinzweig will tell you in his book, "Customer service is not fair." Haven't you been told a million times to suck it up because life isn't fair? Well, learn to live that when it comes to customers. Make sure your customers are treated exceptionally, not fairly.

Bob Dylan had a hit singing,

It may be the Devil
Or it may be the Lord
But you're gonna have to
Serve somebody

When you run a business, you serve your customers. They are your reason for being. Everyone in your company should be committed to making them happy and they should have the authority to do so.

If there's never a problem, there's little opportunity to show your high standards of service. Unfortunately we all make mistakes, and customers do wind up unhappy, sometimes through no fault of our own. Everyone in your business needs to suck it up, bend over backwards, and make the customers ecstatic.

Think I'm beating the subject to death? It's impossible to overstate how important this is. Notice I said you should make the customer *happy*, not *satisfied*. Satisfaction is like living in Purgatory. You may not be unhappy, but you're not necessarily happy either. You may not be hated by your customers but they'll never recommend you to anyone else, either.

COMMODITY VS. BRAND

The dictionary says that a *commodity* is "anything bought or sold." That's way too wide a definition for our use. In business, a commodity is a product or service over which the buyers have most of the influence when it comes to price. Mainly, this is because they see little or no difference between versions of this product or service as it's offered for sale.

On the business side, if you're selling something that consumers see as a commodity, you have little chance of taking business away from your competitor because the only difference the consumer can see is price. Lack of other differentiation almost invariably drives down the selling price. That means you can't make a profit selling (what appears to be) the same damned thing as everyone else.

The easiest differentiation is **name**. That's why you have Joe's Diner, Rita's Diner, Mel's Diner, etc. As long as the named person is some kind of celebrity or is known by the intended customer in some capacity, then they have a chance at getting some of the business in that industry. But as soon as an "outsider" wants to purchase what you and your neighbors are selling, the name difference is negated.

So calling your business "Joe's Web Hosting" will, by itself, get you no customers.

We are programmed to look for differences. In a crowded field of competitors, setting yourself apart in some way is necessary. Ultimately, you are looking to create and direct your *brand*.

Most people can't accurately define what a "brand" is. Most assume that a company's logo, or the proprietary typeface with which its name is spelled is the "brand." Here's a concept most business owners don't seem to want to understand:

A brand exists only in the minds of your consumers, potential consumers, competitors, peers and the public at large. You can try to create and influence your brand, but that's all.

A brand is a shortcut in a person's mind. If I mention the name of a national burger chain (let's call it JesterBurger) to you, all the thoughts, memories and feelings you have about that particular place **is** the brand. Huge corporations try to influence your thoughts and feelings via advertising campaigns, store layout, customer service and a million other interactions. If you are a hard-core vegan, your perception of *any* burger chain is likely to be negative, regardless of how positively they promote themselves and how great your friends feel about eating there.

There are essentially three levels of information gathering. For our purposes, we'll talk about Primary, Secondary, and Tertiary.

Primary information source gathering consists of actually experiencing something (a product or service, in our case).

Secondary information source gathering is hearing about other people's Primary experiences.

Tertiary is – well, everything else.

You walk into a branch of our fictional JesterBurger. You see that the place is clean, the colors are bright, and the people behind the counter are smiling. You order a complete meal and are happy to receive most of your $10 bill back as change. The food appears quickly and the temperature is hot enough that you can assume it was freshly made. You sit in one of the comfortable booths, bite into your JesterBurger Deluxe and decide you enjoy the taste and texture. After finishing your meal, you throw your garbage into the conveniently located can and head for the restroom to wash your hands. You notice that the restroom is well maintained and looks and smells clean. The water is quickly hot enough to wash with soap from the dispenser above the sink, and you air dry your hands with the air jet.

The thoughts and feelings you have about JesterBurger after your visit are from a Primary source – you actually went there and had an experience.

Your friend asks you where you had lunch, and you tell her it was JesterBurger. She's never been there and asks whether you'd recommend it for lunch.

No, you tell her, there was a screaming kid next to you all during lunch. Don't go.

Although JesterBurger has done everything they possibly can to positively influence your experience during your visit, your perception can be influenced by anything and everything during your Primary experience.

Your bad review to your friend is an example of a Secondary source. It's called anecdotal evidence, or Word Of Mouth. When marketing professionals try to create and manage it, they call it Buzz Marketing.

Tertiary information comes from things like media stories, advertisements, marketing materials and other sources. These are usually created, or at least placed, by the subject company trying to influence your thoughts. Similarly the person running JesterBurgerSucks.com has probably loaded their site with negative information and is also trying to influence your opinion.

What does this have to do with defining your brand? You are trying to make certain that your potential client understands what it is that you do, what services you offer, and how you're unique as compared to all your potential competition, all in an instant. You need to focus on a few key things about you and your company that would appeal to potential clients. A simple, representative list might be:

- Location (local vs exotic)
- Services (broad vs narrow)
- Time in businesses (new vs established)
- Ownership (small vs large)
- Design philosophy (simple vs fancy)
- Attitude (funny vs serious)
- Education (6th grader vs PhD)
- Experience (big shop vs entrepreneur)
- Price (low vs high)

If you're in business, you have a brand whether you want one or not. It's your choice to attempt to manipulate it or not. If you do try, what image are you trying to project, and how will you go about it? Again, it's your choice. If you don't attempt to control your brand and make the best impression possible, you are letting your business be seen as totally interchangeable with all the other look-alike web hosts out there.

CUSTOMER SERVICE

At $5 per month or less for web hosting, a company cannot provide active individual customer service and make a profit. FAQ pages and how-to videos are **not** individual customer service. Think about the companies you've dealt with who seem to actively avoid contact with you, offering only voice mail dead ends and an email address that never produces a response.

When it comes down to it, the only thing your customer is buying is customer service. They can get hosting anywhere for less, no matter how low your price is. Again, think about your own experiences with dysfunctional companies. You've probably "voted with your wallet" and gone elsewhere many times when a company ignored your needs and questions.

Think about the business of running a restaurant. A restaurant gets paid for

- Convenience
- Atmosphere
- Preparing food
- Serving food
- Cleaning up afterward

They get paid for anything *but* the actual food! If people only cared about the cost of what they ate, they'd buy the food and stay at home to cook and eat it. People who frequent restaurants expect to pay for service.

If you charge only for web hosting, you will be paid only pennies.

However, when you start providing your customers with

- Service
- Trust
- Reliability
- A warm–and–fuzzy feeling
- A relationship

Then you will start making some serious dollars!

Your service is great as long as nothing is going wrong. It's important how, and how fast, you handle problems.

When there's a serious problem, tell everyone and do it right away. Show your customers that you realize they're in pain and that you're working to resolve it. When everything is fixed, make sure you contact everyone again and let them know. But be humble when letting them know you averted the end of the world single–handedly.

There's a big difference between the old neighborhood beat cop of the 19th and early 20th centuries and today's officers in patrol cars. Cops used to know everyone in their area, talk with them and diffuse tense situations with a stern word or humor before it boiled over into a serious incident. When something bad did happen, the beat cop was looked up to as someone who could be trusted to help out. Today, you often hear people say, "You only see cops when something's wrong," or worse, "There are never any police around when you need them." Don't hide from your customers. A personal e–mail every once in a while lets them know that there's a real person behind the screen. When (not if) hits the fan, they'll be more inclined to treat you like a real person who's helping solve their problems, rather than a faceless entity who caused all their woes.

Communication before, during and after goes a long way towards calming customers during a crap storm.

Having a written plan in place for handling good situations (for instance, getting a referral) and bad ones (a service outage) makes day-to-day operations easier, regardless of the current situation. You should also offer the chance for customers to give you feedback at any resolution point.

Notice I've not used the phrase "customer satisfaction." I don't believe in "satisfying" customers. Satisfied customers have a way of drifting off and become someone else's "satisfied" customers. You need to strive for and achieve "customer wow!" This chapter should get you on the right path.

CUSTOMER-CENTRIC PRICING

Many companies across all industries forget the customer when setting prices for their products and services. Oh, they give lip service to the idea of "How much can they afford? Is the price too low for them to be interested?"

But mostly, the questions raised internally are selfish ones: "What's *our* cost. What's *our* competition's price? Will the owners of *our* company be satisfied with the prices we've set?" These questions can lead to prices that are too high, or worse – too low. They don't really take the real target market into account at all.

Final pricing should not be set based on your cost, or your desired profit margin, but the benefits (financial and otherwise) for your customers.

There was a case study I went over in college that addresses this point exactly. It's available for download from the Harvard Business Review site for around $7. You might want to get it. The link is:

http://hbr.org/product/cumberland–metal–industries–engineered–products–di/an/580104–PDF–ENG?Ntt=%2520pile%2520driving

Briefly, a company creates a new metal disk for using in driving iron piling. One disk replaces dozens of asbestos pads. Given a cost in dollars to make the disk, what should the price for the end user be set at? The quick answer is that it's very high, leaving the company with a huge profit margin. The factors that went into setting the price had nothing to do with the cost of materials or of running *their* business, but about the financial benefits *the end users* reaped from using the new disk.

If you make sure your hosting prices are based on the benefits to your customer, they're easier to explain (justify might be too harsh a word) when talking to prospects. Remember to factor in the *costs* to your clients, not just the *prices* they would pay elsewhere.

Let me tell you a little story about my first foray into web hosting. First you need to understand: all the good advice I'm giving you in this book? I didn't know any of it, and I didn't know anyone to ask for help. So I went in blind, not having a target market, and not knowing what kind of extras I wanted to offer.

I looked at the standard low pricing of the time, $5 per month, and decided I could charge more than that. I tentatively offered my first prospect hosting at $180 per year, prepaid. They jumped on it. Same with clients 2 and 3. Something was wrong here.

Wrong? Yeah. People were taking that price too easily, no selling required. That's when I started thinking about my USP (Unique Selling Point) and crafting the profile for my target market. In a couple weeks, I opened up for new clients again, this time targeting a specific group of people. At twice the price of before.

Bam! More clients jumping in the boat, no selling required. I stopped and looked at what was happening. Because I was laser focused on one group and was speaking directly to their fears and desires, I was able to get them as clients regardless of my new, higher cost.

Since then, I've raised my prices twice. I'm now starting to get some pushback on the prices I'm charging. Does that mean the price is now too high? No, it just means I may have to add in other services to overcome their resistance for the higher pricing.

FYI, this is on shared hosting. I started out paying approximately $200 per year for the space and bandwidth I was reselling, and I made a profit on the very first check I collected every year, with all the rest being pure gravy. Quick calculations show I am now making over 3000% profit on just the hosting. I charge several of my hosting clients much more for additional services.

And here's the deal. I've lost a few clients over the years (my first client fled for someone who charged less than I did, and then had the temerity to ask me for free help on his new site), but I have clients I've been hosting for almost 10 years. If you provide superior customer service to the right target market, hosting clients tend to be very loyal.

Provide your target market with hosting and services at a price they consider to be of value, and you can charge very high prices and realize high profit margins for yourself.

GET CLIENTS BY HAVING CLIENTS

Many businesses open their doors unannounced. The owners think that simply by being there, customers will auto-magically flock to them. Sorry, but this only happens with one-in-a-million businesses, and even those don't usually survive. To use a metaphor, deer won't walk out of the woods and lay in front of you. Not even dumb fish will jump out of the water onto your plate. In order to get customers, you have to have customers.

This is the Catch-22 business owners have been dealing with since civilization began. Since positive word-of-mouth is the best marketing tool ever, how do you get that first customer to take a chance on a brand new, unknown business?

First, never lie about being a new business. Don't try to fool anyone into thinking your company has been around for years when you just opened it last week. Honesty is, as they say, the best policy.

Being a new business can actually be very beneficial. Customers may be more willing to "test drive" your services or simply be enamored of new things in general.

Offer your friends in your target market low cost hosting in return for testimonials and the right to use them in your marketing. You can also approach groups or organizations in your target market with the same offer.

You can also be your own client, or clients. Again, don't try to deceive anyone, but if you're spending a lot of time on line, you've probably got a few interests which could use their own sites. Set them up on your own server, then simply link to them as sites already being served by your new hosting company. If you don't believe in your own service enough to actually use it, why should anyone else?

Once you have a happy client, ask for referrals in your target market. People are often glad to help you after you've helped them. If someone gives you a referral that works out, send them a small token of your appreciation. At minimum a hand-written Thank You note sent via snail mail is essential. (In the age of e-mail and instant digital communication, you wouldn't believe how big an impression these make!) If you do decide to give a gift, make it a small inexpensive one like movie tickets or flowers. Never promise gifts – they should always be unexpected. This adds to their "delight" factor. And never make gifts large or expensive. The recipient may feel you've tried to buy their favor or may feel a sense of obligation.

You can also find a charity that's important to your target market and help them out. Make sure you publicize that help – "Get caught in the act of doing something good," as my friend Tom Shine of HorizonOnHold.com says. Donations of cash or service are nice, but labor – a donation of your time and energy – is often more appreciated and also more likely to gain you publicity.

TEAM UP

It's hard going it alone, especially when you're successful, and you have no one around with whom you can share your tribulations and triumphs. Someone who understands what you're doing, and who can contribute ideas and help.

You don't need to hire employees or take on partners. But if you team up with other professionals and companies that compliment your skill set, ones that serve the same target market yet don't actually compete with you, you can leverage your combined knowledge and experience so that you all get ahead.

Finding these helpers is fairly easy. You need to keep your eyes and ears open and then ask one magic question. You can find potential teammates on line in discussion areas for your target market or via advertisements directed toward them. You can find them at virtual or real-world events held for your target market. A good way is by asking existing customers which other vendors they use in other areas of their business.

You can approach groups and organizations allied with your target market, made up of other people who are already servicing your market. Ask the members who they know, what they do and how they got a foot in the door with people in your market.

You're probably wondering about the "magic question" I mentioned earlier. What is it? How does it work? Well, it's not really magic – it just *seems* that way because so few people think to ask it.

"What can I do for you?"

This question magically opens the door to relationships of all kinds. Most people only ask the selfish, "black hat" version, "What can you do for me?" That question closes doors and shuts off opportunity.

Specifically, you could collaborate with web designers or SEO (Search Engine Optimization) professionals who already service your target market or who would like to. You can team up with insurance agents and real estate agents if your market is home-based businesses. If you host sites for bands and musicians, finding a music store and teaming up with them would be a good start. A local car mechanic might service the fleet of a company you'd like to do work for.

You should be ready and willing to financially support possible team members. No, that doesn't mean loaning them money. If you need their products or services, buy something, cheapskate! Would you want to promote someone who doesn't support you? Neither does anyone else.

If you've already got your foot in the door with your market, find team members that provide products and services your target doesn't realize they need and make a connection. Musicians travel a lot, and need deals on tires, insurance and car repair. Real estate agents need lawn care companies, tree trimmers and contractors to keep listed properties in top shape. Dentists might be looking for office cleaners. You get the idea.

Team members should be actively referring business to one

another, sharing leads. If your team isn't referring to you, you should ask them – and yourself – why not.

Another type of teammate is the freelancer. Yep, you can outsource some of your work to others. While part of the consideration may be cost – that is, can someone else do it for less than if you were to do it yourself – don't be fixated on hiring the lowest-cost provider. Some of the other things you need to think about are speed (How fast can they get the job completed?) and accuracy (When they complete the job, will all the elements be correct?). If you hire someone for the lowest price, and it takes them a month to do a 3-day job, and then it's all messed up anyway, how much have you saved? Nothing! Use freelancers, but get the best you can find at a reasonable cost.

An important source of team members often overlooked? Your own clients! You can swap mentions or links on your sites. You might even offer them discounts or cash rewards for referrals.

Finally, you can build a huge team by starting an affiliate program and turning dozens or hundreds – possibly thousands – of people into a paid sales staff. There are several large affiliate program sites out there and plenty of do-it-yourself software packages that allow you to run your own. You can check ProfitableWebHosting.net's reference page for some suggestions.

TARGET MARKETS

The idea of the Mass Market has been disproved. People aren't some giant conglomerate who do as you hope. There are people who share interests; there are people grouped by demographics. There are niches and sub-niches. Two people who look alike on paper may disagree about everything you think is important.

You want to get to know a certain segment of the general public who not only have the same need but also believe (or can be persuaded to believe) in the same thing. When it comes to web hosting, you could focus on almost any group, as long as you understand that group and are willing to provide services for them. Smokers. Evangelical Christians. Vegans. Female CEOs. It really doesn't matter – you just need to pick a group on whom to focus.

Once you've selected a group you want to service, you need to build a profile for your "ideal customer." Find out what they read, where they hang out and how and where they found out about you. Get to know your ideal customer as if they were a real person – because they are! This person is (or rather, these people are) the ones you're going to go after for your business. You need to know the conversation that's already going on in their heads, and step into it.

The best way to figure out who your ideal customer is is by asking existing customers about themselves. Look for common answers and build a profile out of those.

Let me give you an example that blew my mind when I heard

about it:

In the early days of World War II, the Allies were losing a lot of bombers to the enemy. Hungarian mathematician Abraham Wald took photos of the returning planes and made a composite showing where all the bullet holes were. Then he advised the war department that the bombers needed reinforcing where there were no bullet holes. You cannot add armor all over the plane – it will be too heavy to fly. And if a plane can make it back with bullet holes in the wing, it doesn't need more armor there. *But planes shot in the engine didn't come back, meaning no pictures of planes with holes there, which meant that reinforcements there would have the most effectiveness.*

So, you need to interview existing clients and see where their accounts overlap. That's where you're already doing a good job. Where their accounts don't coincide is where you need to get better at grabbing new clients.

But what about a business that doesn't already have clients? I'm glad you asked.

Again, start building a profile of your ideal customer. Go out and find as many people from within your target group that match the profile and begin to ask them what they need. Ask them what would get them to purchase hosting from you. You may find that you've built an entirely wrong profile or that you need to modify certain part or perhaps feature different services in your offer.

The point is to ask and then to react based on the answers you receive. Be prepared to make drastic changes in your approach in order to get the customers you're after.

TAKING PAYMENTS

Here's a two-fold mind-bending secret. There is no such thing as "business to business" selling. Businesses are made up of people, and the business doesn't decide to do business with you, a person does. Second, although I talk about the "people" in my target market, I'm actually targeting businesses. What I mean is, I don't market my hosting services to individuals who want to run a personal or hobby web site. I market to businesses that are willing and able to pay my higher price points. *My target market specifically includes clients who can help me reach my main goal of providing highly profitable hosting.*

I bill my clients once a year for hosting their sites. I print out hard copies of their invoices and send them off by mail. My bills are net thirty – that is, I give them 30 days to pay the bill in full. Usually within a week I receive a check back in the mail, which I then run down to my bank.

I could just as easily send them an invoice via email, with a link where they could pay with a credit card.

I've even had clients for whom I set up a monthly "subscription" service, where my credit card processor just billed their card every month, and we both forgot about it. This is why I rarely do this. I want my clients to make a decision every year to stay with me. I want them to understand I'm helping them run their business so well that there are no problems.

I've even taken payments in cash. You know, the long green. Benjamins. Again, not very often, but it's happened.

You should decide how you want your clients to pay. Some target markets like paying with a credit card. Others, like most of mine, still prefer to write checks.

At the very least, you need a bank or credit union, someplace that will hold your money until you spend it either by writing a check or making a charge on a card.

If you're going to be collecting funds digitally, you'll need a credit card processor, who should be able to send the funds directly to your bank account. Processors can charge anywhere from a small percentage, usually under 5%, to a percentage of the sale, plus a transaction fee plus a monthly charge to do business with them. Like your own services, the more expensive options may be worth it if they provide you with more and better services than the low priced options.

PayPal is the 800 lb. gorilla of online money collection but there have been reports of frozen accounts and problems getting money out. But they are being challenged by other large companies including Amazon which just released a card reader that will plug into your smart phone or Kindle and allow you to collect funds through them.

My advice is to be ready for any and all forms of payments. I have two digital payment processors, although I rarely use either of them. Again, most of my clients pay by check.

I bill my clients through my legal business, Agile' Marketing Services. My bank account is set up under that name. However, you can collect digital funds as either an individual or as a company of some kind. You may find it easier that way.

That being said, remember that I've urged you to run your hosting company as a business. Do NOT try to avoid paying taxes or try to hide income. Set up a legal business entity and run all of your accounting through it. Aside from any legal problems, taxes help pay for municipal services. If, heaven forbid, your house catches on fire, you don't want the firemen and police not responding because they haven't been paid. Keep it above board.

MONEY MANAGEMENT

The time to plan on what you're going to do with all your money is before you actually start making any. That way you can stick with your plan, make sure all your expenses are covered and find useful and helpful things to do with the profit you're making. The following is a simplified plan for what to do with your gross income.

Note: *Gross income* is the all the money that comes in from your clients. *Net income* is all the money you have left after you pay your required expenses.

- Write out which services are covered by the hosting fee you charge, and which aren't.
- Offer additional services and charge for them.
- Put your incoming money in a bank (a business that will hold and disperse money on demand – bank, credit union, PayPal, etc.).
- Pay your bills promptly.
- Pay yourself a reasonable wage.
- Pay for future charges up front if you can or set money aside for them when you have it (next year's reseller license, customer IP addresses or SSL certificates, etc.).
- Use some money to send unexpected thank-you (cards, small gifts) to clients.
- Use some money to send unexpected thank-you (cards, small gifts) to partners/coworkers/freelancers.
- Use some money (10% – 15% of the net) for other marketing efforts.

• Put aside money for taxes.

• Use 10% – 15% of your net income for upgrading your services or equipment.

• Put money into a SEP (Self–Employed Pension).

PUTTING IT ALL TOGETHER

And here we are, at the peak. This is where are the mysteries are unveiled. Here's where you get the recipe for running the fabled web hosting service that produces a profit.

Many people choose to either work hard or to work smart. I encourage you to do both when following this process. You will make more money, have more fun and help more people.

ONE: You need to be committed to providing a superior customer experience. Those dead or dying hosts littering the Internet I mentioned at the beginning of the book? They thought all it took was to put out sales sites, hook prospects and send them through an automated process. And yes, some people have been lucky enough to make money this way. But it's highly unlikely that *you* will. This process starts and ends with superior customer service.

TWO: Know your target market. I mean intimately. Know what they like, the little details of it all and why they like it. HO gauge model train fans. 1960's Chevrolet muscle car enthusiasts. Left handed piccolo players. The Internet is a wonderland of niches. Find one – the best is probably one you already belong to – and serve that market well.

THREE: Decide what service you will provide that will make you different. What can you offer to your potential clients that they want and that will set you aside from your competitors? This is your position in their minds, your Unique Selling Point (USP). Some people won't want what you feature, and that's fine. You need to finally get it into your brain that not everyone is your target. You actually WANT to discourage some people. If they go away and look elsewhere, then there's more room for the people you actually do want.

FOUR: You can offer your services for a low price, but don't. You want to attract people who can afford your hosting services but who won't be totally dependent on you for everything. This is a business, and you offer hosting services, not daycare or 24–hour nursing. Yes, you want to provide appropriate services, like I mentioned in item One, but you don't want to become their nursemaid. You want to give yourself the financial cushion of being able to provide services when you have to, but not every day and not to all your clients. Offer complimentary services, like web mastering, but be sure you charge for them.

FIVE: You can't do it all on your own. You need to be able to hire freelancers or assistants to help you and to do specialized jobs that you don't handle. Find providers of complimentary services, and set up a referral agreement with them. You have clients who are looking for excellent designers and the designers have clients who are looking for a better web host. Scratch each others's backs. And it doesn't have to be just tech! If you specialize in car club sites, partner with insurance agents, paint companies, parts suppliers – anyone who can provide added value to your clients.

SIX: Most people will not want to do all this. It's work. Not digging–a–ditch work, but work. That means 95% of your competition will remove themselves from your playing field.

SEVEN: The big secret – *you are not selling web hosting!*

What you want to sell is personal service. You want to sell attention, a hands-on contact, that warm and fuzzy feeling. That's where the profit is. The actual hosting is what film maker Alfred Hitchcock used to call "the MacGuffin." It's what everybody thinks they want, but it's not the real focus. Go back and learn – and live – the chapter on Customer Service! As I said, the process begins and ends with superior customer service.

EXAMPLE

Saskia is a senior at her local community college, majoring in acting. Like all the students she knows, she's broke. She's beginning to understand the stereotype of the starving artist! She has a waitress job at one of the local pizza places. The owners are very understanding, but between classes and practicing for the different productions she's in, her work hours are few and far between. She's beginning to think it might be a good idea to have a business of her own that she could run during the odd hours she has free.

One of her friends invites her to a lecture at the college given by a photographer from the bigger city down the highway. Since photography is one of her interests, Saskia decides to go. She takes notes during the lecture and one of the points the photographer makes is that a serious, working photographer needs a good web site, a quality host that supports their clients is worth the premium price they charge.

Saskia remembered a book a friend had on her Kindle, something about running a web hosting business. This might be a business she could run during her off hours! After the lecture, she went up and spoke with the photographer, Teddy. She asked him about his web site and told him about her idea to host sites on the side. Teddy offered to take her to a meeting of the local photography group the following week.

Wanting to be prepared, Saskia looked at her friend's ebook. She visited the companion site, ProfitableWebHosting.net and signed up (using her dad's credit card of course). She's able to go through a number of the lessons on her own time, absorbing most of the basics over the weekend.

The following Tuesday evening, she was at the club meeting with a notebook. Teddy introduced her and explained she was thinking of starting a web hosting businesses for photographers. During the break, she was able to ask several of the members what they wanted in a good web site host. Among the answers she heard were:

- Quality customer service
- Robust site design tools
- Fast servers
- Lots of space
- Someone to talk with who understood their needs
- Free hosting (from one person, who seemed unhappy)

In between classes, practice and two hours of waitressing the next week, Saskia filtered the information she got from the photographers through what she was learning online. She dedicated a notebook to working on her new business venture. She wrote down that her target market right now is professional photographers but she may expand that in the future to encompass all working artists. First, she researched other hosting companies that serve the photography market. She decided her focus will be on providing hosting that offers:

- Large sites for storing photos and video
- Fast server access
- Designers specializing in photo sites

●Promotional support for clients

She decided to offer promotional support because one of the photographers in the group mentioned needing help advertising his services and none of the other hosts seems to offer this.

After doing some research and viewing recommendations, she decided to purchase a small reseller account from HawkHost.com. That meant Saskia needed to design a site of her own. She put a flier up on campus and also searched online for a freelancer who was experienced in art and in web design. She got very lucky! Not only did she find someone online, but there was also a student living on campus who had a small portfolio and was also looking for work.

Between her and her freelancers, Saskia got her reseller site set up in just under a week. She visited the photography department at college. Through a respected instructor, she was able to get three senior students to sign up for hosting at the special rate of $50 for their first year with the promise of positive testimonials if everything panned out. She set up the site spaces quickly and two of the students accepted her offer of design help. The third wanted to design his site himself.

Saskia didn't give up her research. In reading and interacting on WebHostingTalk.com, she met other specialist resellers, confirming her decision that focused hosting was a good side business. One host specialized in sites for multi-office medical practices, another in sites for car dealers, several others offered communities for video gamers, and one woman whose business was hosting Korean language web sites for Korean Americans.

By the time she got back to the photography group two weeks later, Saskia's hosting service had two client sites up and running with a testimonial on her own site from one of the students. She made a short presentation to the group and made two more sales for a year of hosting. This covered all her fixed costs and made Saskia's web hosting business profitable in under one month. Anything else was going to be gravy and the money would go straight towards paying for her education.

Saskia reached out to photography groups in other cities and even to online photography discussion groups. With her growing list of positive reviews and the personal contacts she was making, her side business was growing by leaps and bounds!

FINAL WORD

Well, you've made it to the end of the book. By now, you should be fired up enough to start a first-class web hosting business! You know its work, which is why so many people who believe the "passive income path to millions" baloney have left scrap hosting sites littering the Internet. It's not hard work, mind you, and you can outsource almost all the technical aspects if you want, but it's not a totally hands-off endeavor.

You should be working on your road map, deciding where you are and where you want to go. You should begin thinking about who's going to come along on your trip – employees, freelances and partner businesses.

Think about your USP. See how much interest potential clients have in it. Maybe you got it just right, or maybe you need to change your USP, or the market you're targeting. Be willing to change and adapt. You'll attract different sets of prospects with different offers.

Most importantly, do not strive to have satisfied customers. Don't know what I mean? Go back and re-read the book. In brief: you want customers who are thrilled, overjoyed or some other positive superlative. Anyone can satisfy your customer. And if that's all you're providing – satisfaction – they will probably find someone else to do that at some point.

Thank you for buying and reading this book! I appreciate the time you've shared with me, and I hope you've found *Profitable Web Hosting* enlightening and, well. . . profitable. Use the

Action Items in the next section to get started today!

Very best,

Scott A. Gardner

ACTION ITEMS

1. Research possible target markets: Select several different interest groups that you are familiar with or belong to and learn as much as you can about their web hosting needs and desires.

2. Pick your target market: From the list of interest groups you researched, pick the one you feel you can best support as a hosting reseller.

3. Decide on your unique selling point (USP): What is the one thing that your target market desires that you can focus on doing or providing better than other hosting services?

4. Research reseller hosts and packages: There are dozens of hosts who can provide you with hosting to resell to your direct clients. Decide what you need and what price point you can afford.

5. Name your business and register your domain name: Pick a name that will tell your target audience that you're in business for them and then register that name with a registrar.

6. Create your reseller site: Once you purchase your reseller package, either begin creating your hosting site yourself or hire someone to do it for you. Think about what would attract your target market as you design it.

7. Decide on your packages and pricing: Think about the levels of hosting you want to provide your target market and what you should include or exclude from each, along with price points which will help you achieve your goal of running a profitable web hosting company.

8. Find complimentary services and invite them to partner: What kinds of services will you need in order to run your business? What services or products can you offer your target market? Find suppliers (businesses or freelancers) who can provide these and offer their services through your business.

9. Start a basic balance sheet: Just a simple spread sheet where you keep track of money you're spending and money that's coming in.

10. Write a basic marketing plan: Who do you want to reach? How do you want to reach them? What can you do for free? For a low cost? For a higher cost? What kinds of clients will these efforts reach? What is your projected ROI (Return On Investment)? Actual ROI? When will you do these marketing efforts?

Review your efforts and results, compare against your goals and readjust. Follow your existing or modified marketing plan and make those efforts again.

RESOURCES

Reseller Sources:
HawkHost.com
BlueHost.com
FatCow.com

Registrars:
GoDaddy.com
PowerPipe.com
NameCheap.com

Freelancers:
Fiverr.com
Guru.com
eLance.com

FREE PREVIEW: MEMBERSHIP SITE DESIGN

Why Wordpress?

Wordpress was created as blogging software – a sort of on-line journal. And it still functions wonderfully as such! But Wordpress can also be used as a Content Management System (CMS), allowing someone who knows nothing about coding or working with web sites to actually run one.

There are two versions of Wordpress. The first one, located at Wordpress.com, allows you to set up a blog on their site for free and run it. The address will be something like "MyFantasticBlog.Wordpress.com ." You can give this address out freely and visitors can come here and read your profound words of wisdom.

The other site, Wordpress.org, allows you to download the software and install it – again at no charge – to your own web site. You can customize your Wordpress installation with all sorts of add-ons.

Many people choose Wordpress to build their site around because it is free, and relatively easy to figure out. There are thousands of Wordpress sites installed around the world, in dozens of languages, and thousands of certified and non-certified experts who can help you do almost anything with it.

The software itself is fairly plain. It allows you to create pages, and set up one specific page for showing your blog posts. But it has many "hooks," or places that developers can add in software that does specific jobs. Membership software is one such type of plug-

in. You can also get your site translated into other languages, add i[n]
calendars where visitors can schedule their own appointments with
you, add in discussion boards. . . literally almost any modification
you can think of, it's already out there, in probably a dozen differen[t]
versions.

Your posts, which are probably where a lot of your membership
content will be stored, are meant to be text-based. But you can als[o]
add audio or video content to them, and attach files for display or
download. You can give your members a true multi-media learnin[g]
experience quite easily.

For the purposes of this book, we're going to suggest that you
register your own domain name and install the latest version of
Wordpress to the root directory. Registering a domain name will
probably cost you about $15 per year. Web hosting space can rang[e]
from $5/month to several hundred dollars per year, depending on
how robust the host is, and how much help and what types of
services they offer.

We're not going to offer a walk-though for Wordpress installatio[n]
and administration here. Please check the *Links* chapter near the
back of the book for help with this and other instructions that are
beyond the scope of this book. No worries – we've hooked you

Uses Of A Membership Site

A membership site can be used for almost any reason imaginable. There are as many different types of membership sites as there are reasons for joining one. This book focuses on creating educational or learning sites; sites that consist mainly of content behind a membership "wall" that are meant to teach the members new or interesting information, concepts or knowledge.

This specialized information can be lumped together, or broken up into segments or levels (courses). Simple sites will allow the member to access all the information at once, and trusting them to work through it in order, at their own speed. A more complex site can be set up to "drip" the contents to a user at given intervals, like a given number of days apart, or when they've indicated that they finished one lesson and are ready to move to the next one.

The main purpose of membership software is to provide a wall keeping general site visitors out, while allowing recognized individuals – members – to access restricted content. Again, this book is about sites that teach, but the restricted content could be a collection of digital content, or even just an areas where people with a shared interest can chat back and forth. If you think about it, music streaming sites like Spotify and Pandora are just huge membership sites with a customized way of accessing the restricted content.

One of the best reasons for having a membership site is to keep a list or database of all the members and their contact information. You can track who is seeing the restricted content, and keep in touch with them to let them know about revised content, new lessons, and so forth. Verified contacts, especially ones that have proven they want your information, are an important sales resource.

Here are just a few of the types of membership sites that you might set up:

- Coaching or consulting

- Digital collection access

- Clubhouse

- Social or political groups

- Specialized education

- Collaborative work

- *And many, many more!*

We're not going to tell you what type of site to set up, and you certainly don't have to stop with just one. Feel free to experiment The information in this book can help you with almost any type o restricted access site you want to set up.

As you begin to design your site, you want to keep the end in mir What do you want each user to do once they've completed a course? Perhaps you have higher levels of information they can access at the same site. Perhaps you want to move them into a me intensive and costly program. Or perhaps you simply want to let them hang around for as long as they like. Any of these options is fine. After all, it's your site. With learning sites, we find that thes are perfect vehicles for moving members into other programs. Ju be ready to design an ending for your members, as needed.

Before You Begin

There are a number of questions you should ask yourself as you begin to jot your design ideas down. The very first one is: Should I be using a membership site at all? There are options for simpler systems, like putting your content in a password protected directory and giving out the one password to as many people as there are who want to access that information. I have a client who does that with the presentations from their annual conference.

If you're putting together a number of courses, or you want several courses created and taught by different instructors, a more robust teaching platform, like Moodle, might be appropriate. It's designed to offer different types of content, administer quizzes, and produces number or letter grades for each student on completion of a course.

Another consideration is time. Do you want to give start a bunch of students at the same time, or can a student start whenever they want? Can they access all course materials at once, and complete it at their own pace, or will you drip content out at certain intervals?

What do you want to teach? If this knowledge is something only you know, then you're stuck having to come up with the course contents on your own. Maybe you've already written a book, or series of articles. Maybe you created a video program. You can re-craft the information into different lessons, different courses. Or you may pull information from other sources, other authors or creators. A text file from one person, an audio interview with another one.

You also need a target market. This is the group of people to whom you want to advertise your membership site, people who might be interested in joining. If you know the type of content you want to offer, this should give you a good idea of the target market. Advanced skateboarding lessons aren't likely a good fit for most senior financial analysts, while most tween girls aren't interested in a course about applying horror movie special effects make-up.

You should begin making a list of the general and specific content you want on the site, and how you're going to structure it, by lessons and by courses. How will this content be presented? Will it be text-based? On-line only? Or will you allow members to download files like PDFs, and audio or video files? Do you have all the hardware and software you need to generate this content, and to make it available to your members?

Do you have the time and experience to administer all the lessons, courses, and levels on your own? If not, you can either recruit or hire one or more people to help you. I help run a (non-membership) Wordpress-based restaurant review site that has several people logging in to write reviews, a couple editors who can proofread the text reviewers leave, and two administrators who can push the button to publish the content on the site.

You also need to decide if you will charge for access to the membership area. I know there are several dozen books out there claiming you can make a million dollars with a membership site while sitting back and doing nothing. This is not one of those books! However, you can charge for access and make some coin if you successfully reach the correct target market. You can have a mix of membership levels; the first level may give some general information for free (in exchange for valid contact information, which can be worth more than what you'd charge for access to the information), and the higher levels give more specialized information in exchange for payment.

As far as taking payment, there are many credit card processors out there you can sign up with. Many charge a percentage of each transaction, plus a small set fee per transaction. Some even levy a monthly charge to process your payments. Then there are others like PayPal and Stripe that charge you per transaction, and that's it. Even Amazon has opened their own on-line payment service. [NOTE: not all membership site software programs hook into all payment processors. You'll need to check with each one and see if it can handle your processor of choice.]

A basic Wordpress installation, plus some basic text-based content, should take up less than 100 MB of space on your host's server. However, unless you know you won't be taking up that much space, I'd recommend going with at least 250 MB of space. This gives your site room to grow, and to store lesson content. I ***do not*** recommend going with a host who offers you "unlimited space." Remember, they're offering that to each and every one of their other customers too, and some of them are going to take as much space as possible. More importantly, they will also take the computing power of that server, leaving you with a slow-running site.

If you're going to be serving video content as part of your lessons, space and speed are additional considerations. I would, however, suggest you store your videos on another site instead. Having some content on YouTube is great, but then everyone has access to that, registered member of your site or not. I'd put certain videos, like the welcome video for your free section, on YouTube where it will be indexed and reported on Google and other search engines, where people can trip over it and find you. There are cloud services like

Amazon's S3 service, or Google Drive, where you can store your videos, and Vimeo has semi-pro and professional options as well. I'd investigate those and choose the one best suited for our needs.

Each page on your site, and every post, has the option for readers to comment. Many membership plug-ins either restrict this automatically, or offer you the option of doing this on each post and page. If you want to interact with your members, or if you want them to interact with one another, letting them comment on each post or lesson is the simplest option. However, if you want to foster deeper discussions, and offer them more options for commenting – or just to natter back and forth – installing a forum plug-in might be the way to go. These require some additional setup on installation, and they're another thing you or someone else is going to need to administer. However, for certain types of sites they can be invaluable.

Many sites now offer badges to members. A badge is simply a small picture that shows the user has finished some task. The Open Badges project web site is probably the best place to learn all about these. You can install a plug-in that awards badges to users upon completion of a lesson, course or level. Badges are still relatively new out there, and changes are taking place rapidly. If they're something you want to offer your members, it's best to stay up on the current discussions about them, and keep your software updated.

Speaking of finishing, you should have a plan for how you want the course or level to end. Maybe it's a lesson that ties together all the other information you've presented. Perhaps it's an interactive lesson where they show off what they've learned. Maybe it's just simple message of congratulations, or the awarding of a certificate license. Maybe you have higher levels you want them to move to that's how many of the sites I set up end most levels or courses. Whatever it is, you should beginning planning for it now, and figure out how you want to present this to your members.

Once you've answered all of these concerns for yourself, you'll be about 80% done with the planning process.

* * * * *

Buy the *Membership Site Design* ebook now – only $3.99

http://amzn.to/1nD937S

ACKNOWLEDGEMENTS

This book would not exist in a readable form without the help of two master proofreaders. I owe them more than I can possibly say.

Sharon Linne is an English instructor at not one, but **TWO** colleges. She knows what she's talking about, and she helped me sound lucid and aware.

Charles McGraw (www.CGMcGraw.com) is a published author with several speculative fiction titles under his belt. He was the cofounder of the now-disbanded Fantastic Fiction Forum writer's group, home to several nationally-published authors. He forced me to take a scalpel to my work, and it is now much healthier.

And without the love and support of my wife Arlene Staubsinger, I simply would not exist as the person I am today.

REGISTRATION

I want to sincerely thank you for purchasing my book *Profitable Web Hosting*. If you found it useful, I'd ask that you do a couple things.

First, please register your copy at this address –

http://profitablewebhosting.net/book-registration/

This will add you to a mailing list I keep ONLY for informing my readers about new books, or about major revisions to books I've published. You'll get a welcome email, and then emails only when I put out a new book.

Second, please take a moment to leave a review on-line at:

http://amzn.to/1zeox8D

I hope if you found the book useful you'll leave a 4– or 5–star review.

Now, get to work on those Action Items and start building your web hosting business today!

37072980R00064

Made in the USA
Lexington, KY
16 November 2014